Shahr-e-jaanaan sets out to recreate the universe of Urdu and Persian poetic tradition, its tropes both lenses and mirrors for the speaker's reality. As she maps her romances onto legends, directing their characters perform her own tragedy, their fantastical metaphors easily lend themselves to her fluctuating mental state. Cycling between delirious grandeur and wretched despair, she is torn between two selves— the pitiable lover continually rejected, and the cruel, unattainable beloved comparable in her exaltation to a god. *Shahr-e-jaanaan* explores, interrogates, and distorts these dichotomies and their symbolism, calling into question the forces that elevate some to divinity even as they damn others to injustice and oppression.

"The only way for any literature to grow is to be in conversation with other traditions, other voices. Where would the intricate and deeply moving tradition of English sonnets be without Sir Thomas Wyatt and Henry Howard's bringing it from Italy in the 16th century? Or, more recently, where would we be without Agha Shahid Ali's passionate pursuit of ghazal in English, expanding American tradition in ways that no one could have predicted. Adeeba Shahid Talukder enters this conversation between traditions with elegance and insight. Herein we discover Urdu poetics of giants as different as Mirza Ghalib and Faiz Ahmed Faiz, gently brought into English by Talukder's own hand. Opening this book in the middle— starting with short lyrics such as 'The Scaffold's Branch' and 'Exotica'— I was immediately taken with their elegance of striking yet tender tonal shifts. Then, I dove into the the longer poem, 'On Beauty,' marveling at its integrities of the unsaid, its singing, its questions. This is one of those books that truly teaches us how to read it. After everything we thought we knew about the moon, herein is a chance to see it with new eyes. After everything we thought we knew about ourselves, and our loss, there is more to find: 'When the color left / my cheeks,' the poet writes, 'You / left too.' This book is an exquisite lyrical feast."
— Ilya Kaminsky, author of *Deaf Republic* and *Dancing in Odessa*

"Beauty and urgency, lyricism and violence are carefully orchestrated into conversation. The beauty of these poems arises from their complexity, the infinite ways they bring together lyricism and urgency, femininity and violence, adornment and danger. 'In this intricacy is power.' This is a first book you will not soon forget."
— Kristina Marie Darling, author of *Dark Horse: Poems* & Editor-in-Chief of Tupelo Press

"Adeeba Talukder's *City of the Beloved* hovers on the nexus of heartache and joy, a meeting point of arrival and exodus, and where love is the revolving door to the world of the unknown. Recalling the concision and scintillating acumen of Emily Dickinson, Mirabai, Rabia and Sappho, and drawing on the masters of Urdu and Persian poetry, Talukder renders a full world of heart, soul, and body, profound and daunting, sensual and sacred, enchanting and redeemable. This is a beautiful, stunning and unforgettable book."

— Khaled Mattawa, author of *Mare Nostrum*

"I stayed in a perpetual state of goosebumps while reading Adeeba Talukder's debut collection, *Shahr-e-jaanan*, no lie. Maybe because the settings evoked are familiar and tangible but also magical, otherworldly. Maybe it's that I fell captive to the spells of its stories—Scheherezade and her command over wild nights of imagination come to mind. Maybe it's the way Talukder manages to both evoke Urdu poetic tradition and create her own—these poems swoon with the restrained sensuality of the old world while dancing with the glittering passions of the new. Let yourself get caught up in this book's wondrous whorls and whirls—you won't regret it."

—Tarfia Faizullah, author of *Registers of Illuminated Villages* and *Seam*

SHAHR-E-JAANAAN:
THE CITY OF THE BELOVED

شہرِ جاناں

ADEEBA SHAHID TALUKDER

T|P

TUPELO PRESS
North Adams, Massachusetts

Shahr-e-jaanaan: The City of the Beloved.
Copyright © 2020 Adeeba Shahid Talukder. All rights reserved.

Library of Congress Cataloging-in-Publication data available upon request.

ISBN: 978-1-946482-29-7

Cover and interior designed by Howard Klein.

Cover art: Haji Madni, "Marriage Procession of Dara Shikoh," circa 1740-50, Oudh State, Provincial Mughal, Tempera on paper, 23 x 15 inches. National Museum, Delhi.

1st edition: March 2020

.

Tupelo Press
P.O. Box 1767, North Adams, Massachusetts 01247
Telephone: 413-664-9611 / Fax: 413-664-9711
editor@tupelopress.org / tupelopress.org

Tupelo Press is an award-winning independent literary press that publishes fine fiction, non-fiction, and poetry in books that are a joy to hold as well as read. tupelo Press is a registered 501(c)(3) non-profit organization, and we rely on public support to carry out our mission of publishing extraordinary work that may be outside the realm of the large commercial publishers. Financial donations are welcome and are tax deductible.

NATIONAL ENDOWMENT for the ARTS
arts.gov

Supported in part by an award from the National Endowment for the Arts.

Preface

Many of the poems in this collection occur in dialogue with Urdu poetic tradition. I reference and pay homage to several poets throughout this book— among them Mirza Ghalib, Mir Taqi Mir, Faiz Ahmed Faiz, Allama Iqbal, Mirza Sauda, Noon Meem Rashid, Ibn-e-Insha, and Agha Shahid Ali. I have lived with these poets' verses for so long that I know them by heart; they permeate my consciousness and are lenses through which I view the world, through which I write.

The title of the final section of this collection is a reference to Mohammad Husain Azad's 1880 book of Urdu literary history, *Ab-e-Hayat*. The work embodies the British denunciation of the ghazal as decadent, immoral, and contrived due in part to the fantastical tropes and imagery that form its universe. After years of studying ghazals and dwelling within this very space, I seek to defend and decolonize this universe— its beauty, its grandeur, its intellectual feats. At the same time, I defy the patriarchy of it, the patriarchy with which so much of literature is cursed.

All translations, where they occur, are my own. Some are transcreational, and are based on the way the particular verses converse with the themes of my poems.

Arms wild, intoxicated, dancing,
with dust-smeared heads and bloodied shirts—
come! The City of the Beloved waits.

—Faiz Ahmed Faiz,
    Let us today enter the bazaar in shackles

Table of Contents

v. The Tearing

vi. Shahr-e-jaanaan: The City of the Beloved

vii. god vs. God

viii. The Water of Life

for my beloved,
Willem

When in the dark / my mind brightened

I realized I could no longer
wait to be beautiful. Thus, I pushed
bangles upon bangles
onto my wrist, rubbing
my hands raw with metal
and glass.

Each time a bangle broke, I watched
the blood at my veins
with a grim face,
feeling more like a woman.

No symmetry or sequence.
All colors clanged upon my arms,
bright, jeweled, and dissonant.

That night, my mother
looked into my eyes with terror.
That night, she wouldn't let me leave.

i. The Wine Cup

The Lightning of Glory should have fallen
on me, not on Moses.

Pour as much as the drinker can hold.
— Ghalib

the mosque an eyebrow, the tavern an eye

When on the fifteenth night
the moon began to wane,
centuries of copper,
of gold,
of marbled wrists

glinted once, then found the sand.

That night, no poets came
to the gatherings of the fair-faced,
no drunkard was banished
from their lanes.

All candles fell quiet.
The beloved hung on dry branches,
perfumed, silvering.

There was
no god.

In all the sky,
there was no God.

"The sky is moving, the sky is moving!"

The toddler's scream tore the air, unsettled Washington Square. His sister danced around him, eyes open into cold: *"Where is it coming from? Where is it moving to?"*

"It's moving! The sky is moving! Oh birds, birds! Don't leave!"

Clouds raced out of the square, trailed by pigeons. Their black shadows slipped off the clock tower, then returned, flapping madly.

"Birds, please stay! Stay, sky!"

They swooped under, circled twice, then moved further into the sky.

Crossing Manhattan Bridge

Beads of light,
the curve of the rosary
the sky bleeding stains of henna—

they always block the sun,
the East River.
They refuse to sway,
leaning hard against the metal.

Splinters of orange
between thick hairs,
their faces on fire.

We roll across the track
like cracks of thunder
high above the breaking

branch, its red leaves spilt
across the moon.

Fall fast to prostrate.

My eyes
the depth
of darkness, darkness.

Ammi

My mother whispered verses over water,
left large knives beneath our beds
to rid us of her own evil eye.

Half-bitten suns appeared.

They could not soothe us to sleep,
revealed silences
too slippery to be sewn.

We mistook the cracks in her voice for fissures.

Stayed numb and nude.
Each pang of reverence
pressed beneath our marbled skins.

Under the heart's flaming core we sat
picking needles
when we could have plucked

stars from the sky.

You're getting older, and there are such few boys.

My mother tells me this in the mornings over FaceTime, brow furrowed, washing all the dishes. Sometimes, her voice breaks.

She says I shouldn't be living alone, with no one to care for me when I get into one of my moods, or have a cold. It gets dark, too, so early, she says.

You're getting older, and there are such few boys.

★   ★   ★

Ammi, you've always been so soft. Smiling wide and almost smacking your lips when you tell me stories of the prophets, of how God graced them, how evil was undone.

In Greenwich Village there are satans, you say. Men who practice witchcraft and mix alcohol into your water.

There was a night when we could not find you, and I knew someone had tied knots in your hair. It was so cold that night, and we found you at last in Roosevelt Island, dancing on the rocks. You laughed and laughed, said you would feed all the fish in the river. Who, now, will marry you?

You're getting older, and there are such few boys.

ii. The Nightingale

In place of oil, passion pours
the nightingale's blood into the lamp of the rose.
—Mir

Quicksand

"I've only seen your ear once,"

he said somberly.

His heart was of buttons and string.

This was January, when

all the world was snow.

This morning is white, the sun

frozen behind clouds.

"There was a time I did not tell you,"

he says, smiling at the branches

like ink streaks across the sky.

"We were in your home

and your hair spilled

out of the cloth and curled

to your cheeks.

I considered telling you,

but told myself instead:

No, that would be strange.

Be quiet, just drink

your rose drink."

He dances over the cracks in the sidewalk but cannot hide from her gaze.

He knows, with his half-smile and shaded eyes and the honey running

through his veins.

Farhad the Mountain Carver

He swept all magic from her windows, closed the blinds so the crows would not come in. Wove her stories to cloak his hideous face. Gave her roses in the winter, crimson with a nightingale's blood.

> The footprints in the lake stretched
>
> to the other side, with no hint of water.
>
> You reached for my hands,
>
> watched my breath stop.

Shireen wore a ring, lived deep in the mountains. Her king was away at war for months. *Farhad*, he told himself, *it is time to carve channels of milk into stone.*

> *Tilt your head,* you told me.
>
> In the darkness I learned: the ice
>
> in the grass blades
>
> could look like stars.

As evening fell he beat his drum so hard his cheeks flushed. *I own you,* she told him. He knew. That night he cut a lock of her hair, dyed it purple as she slept.

Fanaa: End of Self

A glance was all it took
to turn him mad as a moth—

Majnoon,
unbathed and barely clothed,
teeth chipped, lips hard,
hair and hair
ran through the bazaar,
ripped his collar, cried
Laila, Laila

Dust on his head, blood
on his sleeve,
he danced
as the Gods of the Age
cast stone after stone
upon his chest.

Her curls, too,
had once fallen on him
like calamity. Now he tore

the desert with verses
of thirst and praise:
Come, quell my fever.
Even death is not so cruel.

As she rose again
she was smoke, soft
and gray, searching.
His wings,
by now, were burnt.

You've destroyed me, he accused.
And when she wrote at last,

he ingested her words,
smashed their shrines.

Hourglass

upon the heart's throne:
Sun, its glimmer
vanishing dew before dark

        milky-throated
        moonless sky, stretches and stretches
        of skin unkissed

years of light
between evenings

    fall.

After eating her letter

his throat
is crawling.

Laila.

Her name
in the flushed
dark:

fragrant,
heavy as air,

pressed

rose petals
in the pages
of a book.

Their thin velvet,
the periphery dark,

brittle.

He throws the silk
over her shoulder.

Its blue
glides down.

Subh-e-firaaq:
Morning of Separation

You're a saint, the mountain carver
told the lonely Shireen. More even
than stone.

He carved for her,
almost

a stream of milk. Then threw
himself off.

Fell, his limbs
with the leaves he clutched.

iii. **In Shackles**

for Majnoon
—*after the 1976 Hindi film Laila Majnu*

Death is not so cruel.

Does the nightingale not see
the bleeding rose, how she tears
her collar, her very flesh?

He is mad, she pleads. He is mad.
I am to blame: It was I
who stole his senses.
Stone me,
bring me to the scaffold.

Come once,
just once
to see her forehead
clear as a mirror
rubbing itself into dust.

Show the Gods of the Age
that the world is not full of snow.

The Holy Men

They told him then:
you are not vast.

You are nothing

but gashes
from the stones

that pelt you, thick
torrents of her

locks. You, exiled,
broken-winged,

will stay
wandering, nowhere.

Your verses will rip
the air but find

no one. Know this:
if she were god,

she would answer.

Mansur the Heretic

There, he let slip his robe
and they all knew:

   his flesh was God.

The sky split, mountains fell
as he hung in the sky,
gleaming like wine.

That night, Revolution walked
to the gallows—
lips red, hands silver,
            curls like black rain.

His heart, she found,
was ash.

She circled it seven times,
then fell, flaming,
at his feet.

In Exile

His feet
on so many sands. His blisters

white as pearls.

He sees the turning angel,
touches her skin,

finds
her lips pale.

In her wrist
the pulse of water.

the branch

Majnoon, his collar sewn,
                    returns to the city.

He scatters the petals of roses, dark
like the horizon.

In the courtyard, a child eats dust.

for Qays

—a transcreation of Sauda

Come walk with me
by the lake's empty benches.
Tell me, dressed in roses

                we need some air.

The wound's head has reached the heart—
there's no use in sewing it or rubbing it with balm.

All the lovers have snuffed their lamps,
headed back over the broken paths.

Said Sauda in madness:
what has passed, has passed.
We lovers who court calamity
deserve it all.

5 Poems

undulate
The east river is never still upon stones and ships.

tremble
Always, the chance of touch.

leaf
How thin we are— how even a breeze
makes us flap, snap, fall.

crooked branches before night
They are like hands frozen into longing,
hairs tangled beyond separation.

Urdu
A Delhi courtesan adorned to madness,
weeping Ghalib.

If It Were

—after Ghalib

The hospital sheets cover my face. No one sees. My eyes are closed, my hands spread like a hem. The walls white like jasmines.

    I sing: *I would die happily, if it were once.*

The patients' quarters are hushed but I can hear his breathing, the way he smiles into my neck and ear. In each room, his bulk rises and falls beneath the thin blankets. In each room, his face in the blue light. I scream and scream.

    His arrow was half-drawn. The liver aches, anticipating its touch.

The scale cannot measure my weight. I am a goddess; the sickle moon and East River are mine to feed. I shred all the roses, let the torn petals fall all over the tiles.

★ ★ ★

A building in the skyline blinked red. I rushed into lobbies with lipstick on my chin, asked where I was. They just stared. Outside it was cold and my sandals clapped the rocks.

I sang until midnight. He didn't come.

iv. The Courtesan

A sigh needs a lifetime to take effect;
who will live until your curls are conquered?
—Ghalib

Episode

She started as a dot. One could know her just by observing the space around her. Except when she had company— then, they couldn't discern her at all. It was difficult being a dot— she wasn't so aware of where she began or ended. She couldn't stand up straighter than herself.

Robert Hayden once wrote a poem about a father whose hands cracked into the splintering cold. She often thought about what it meant for cold to splinter. She shook off the lies she'd gathered over the years. Combed the rest out of her hair.

All the women sliced their wrists when they saw Yusuf's handsome face. They'd been holding the knives for apples. They started spitting excuses. We will continue our lives, they resolved. Grandmother sat in chains. The system was tailored to aesthetes. Light upon aluminum. Its glint as far as days.

Most sharp things end with a point. She experienced cravings of nine: nine shoes, nine pens, nine pencil points, nine men who believe it is okay to sit with their legs wide apart.

One night, she performed the dance of the courtesans. They came up and handed her bits of ginger candy, asked her to interpret the tattoos on their arms. She twisted her wrist and spun until she did not know who she was.

They did not know how to tear their collars. She left them without a country to weep in.

The night of the fourteenth
—*after Ibn-e-Insha*

All night, *jaanum,* they sing
of you—

your cypress
sway,

your cheeks of silver.
*Tell u*s, they say,

how black is her curl?
> *did you, Insha, pick*
> *her thorns?*

I laugh—
> the veil is threadbare

yet. Let it darken
longer.

On Courting Calamity

—after N.M. Rashid

A thread

from pre-

eternity

to past time's

end, a thread

that binds

movement

to gesture, a crow

to a narcissus.

I stretch.

My waist, this morning,
is a knot.

Because she could not

find the water
under the hills
or in the creek
in the yard—

the rocks sat
alone in the air
and the moss, too
lay parched—

she stole
garlands from boat
bows, marigolds
pressed together on thin
white cord, jasmines
and roses still wet
with dew,

crushed them
until they dripped
from her fingers.

Asymptote

I don't understand why some bearded boys
insist on keeping all their hairs—

> at some point you must part
> with what is not
> beautiful,
> what cannot be
> contained
> in the moon's tilting
> glass.

>> If all was light
>> the mountains would crumble.
>> If all was God (even golden calves and ancient testicles)

Mansur would not have hung,
Aaron
would not have had his hair
pulled to shame.

the quiver of her red
lips
his heart
a throne

in pieces

would be

one

not

Too
faR
too   di

s   tract   Ed

to   be
wiEld (ed)

Ah!

—after Ghalib

Longing, air-spent
travels the length of age, then receives
a faint reply:

You have conquered a curl, at last.

Long,
how long I've traveled your tresses,
their black thick as night
forest of tangled twisting thoughts:

hip to waist,
along the length of the back
to the neck—made of softest light—
but before I could reach your temple's summit,
my breath collapsed.

I fell, clutching just a lock of your hair.

Mumtaz Sahib of the Round Glasses

I

On the train back
from the meeting, he stroked
his peppered hair:

With you I feel
I am with
a flower.

your eyes
are like nuts—
like almonds.

I laughed.
He looked
at the subway floor,
placed a breath strip
on his tongue.

II

The 23rd Street platform
was empty. There he stripped
metaphor from love:

My skin gleamed like the moon.
My hair was made of clouds.
My lips were petals
of a rose.

    My eyes were lakes at night.

He wanted to plunge
into them, naked.

III

As the train left his thick hands closed
around my waist.
He leaned in, panting
give me a kiss, come
kiss me.

His beard hairs against my cheek.
My skin burning beneath his hands.

III

Have I upset you?
You will come to my apartment
and we will watch a movie and you
will forget.

Please reply to my texts. I have
many famous friends.

I hope I have not done something
to make you angry. You are like
my daughter, like my daughter.

Friendship is like a pearl. How will
I find another one?

IV

Dear Adeeba,

I have found another translator.
Please return my short stories.

Respects,
Mumtaz

Kathak: The Dance of the Courtesans

i.

In the mirror, tilt
your chin
        higher.

At the end of each
chakkar, return to your own
               eyes.

Your breath, a spool of thread—
thin, sharp,
unravels. Pull, pull
           it back in.

Shackle yourself until
        your ankles
are gold;
        hold your wrists
delicate
beneath your jewels.

Now dance; the city awaits you.

ii.

Goddess, beloved, flame, they say:
all beauty converges in you.

Men gather at saints' tombs,
but rush to your doorstep

with greater madness.
Let them gaze at you

until you begin to tremble;
allow yourself to be slight-

ed. You, fragile
as glass, will learn:

you were made   to break.

iii.

In the final scene of the 1972 Hindi film *Pakeezah*, Meena Kumari's love
is getting married to someone else, and she is performing at the wedding.
She shatters a lamp, then dances upon its shards, leaving crimson foot-
prints all over the white sheets.

v. The Tearing

Of Water

I lay thin, a carcass in the low wind and blue night. The air moving between my ribs, shoulder blades and sky.

I found him in the skin between his hairs, pale and molting. He held it up with just two fingers, chin and mustache spilling from his hands.

How quietly they leave the plates on the wooden ledges, with crumbs that have touched their lips. As though it were nothing at all.

At the end of this street, Washington Square is white— its lamps empty, its bushes translucent. The chess players are shadows. They no longer call me Princess.

To Heaven

Wrap a fence around your dream of white.

Walk a cord thin as a hair.

Splinter the sun, wake all its ashes.

A Robe of this World

Look! God descends   like fog

   upon the city,   clouding

      mirror,   horizon—

          offering little

more than the illusion

     of dream.   The parched

        hold their tongues   to the air,

        heavy with water.

★ ★ ★

Smash your idols, He says.

We throw ourselves
          at His feet,   shatter

    for the musk- scented,   rose- colored

       wine of heaven.

★ ★ ★

I see myself   in the bright   crystal of the stream,

slender, sharp.   The water rubs its forehead   in clay,

cuts itself until it flows red.

★ ★ ★

The first three weeks of war

Someday I will forget
to think of you.

Like a fawn drinking water,
the azure disappearing beneath her tongue.

The coming of spring
—after Faiz

He found in the leaves
a mixture of dread and shaking
        hands. The patient smiled
        just once before death.

The lake flowed in the wind
like a river and there
        the skies smelled like Pakistan
        of all the bloodied feet washed
        in the water.

They taunted him still,
asked why he had
        hennaed his toes, why in this
        dawn he'd not had a scrap to eat
        of the sky.

The answer was in the moths:
they had gorged
        on dawn's yellow
        ornaments and filled jewels.

Now they darkened the sky
and tore its flesh
        and the cold water, too,
        tore into every niche
        of light.

He had searched the horizon
again and again.
        She wasn't there.
        There were no angels.

For J.R.

Between leaves and apples
they found you:
tall, thin, some inches of skin
clinging to your teeth.
Your glasses of charred wire,
bits of your shirt
still plaid, bits of you
rising with the autumn air.

Nayyara Noor's voice scaled and descended the Khamaaj
as we put your face on lamp posts. All evenings fell
with your pawned blood on the streets.

Surpass fear or let life pass us by—
to die or to live: this matter's still in the air.

The rain left bare the scented candles,
let flow the words of poems,
the large R.I.P. Josh,
your face, sketched in pencil,
lying under the roses.

It was a December without jazz gigs.
We cracked peanuts and listened quietly
as the trombone wept like a truck.

When in the dark/ my mind brightened (revisited)

Each time a bangle broke, I watched
the blood at my veins
with a grim face,
feeling more like a woman.

That night, the window air was open,
the full moon luminous. I waited
for my mother to turn, to see me
as a bride.

I wanted to tell her:

The world is adorning itself
for my wedding.

That night, my mother looked
into my eyes with terror. That night,
she wouldn't let me leave.

vi. Shahr-e-jaanaan:
The City of the Beloved

At December's end Benazir died
in a suicide attack.

Men burned

tires, cars, banks,
petrol pumps, and factories,

perhaps in grief.

The nights in New York
were clear, cold

and I read Faiz
in a way I never would

again. In Washington Square,
the benches were empty.

The trees without leaves,
their branches thick

enough to hang
something.

★ ★ ★

That winter I found myself

in His apartment,
wearing so many bangles

they couldn't move
or make a sound. He gave

me a glass of water, walked me
to his bedroom.

I said *marry me first.* We spoke
our vows. He couldn't

pronounce the Urdu.

* * *

An hour later, he told me
he didn't love me, said

not to take it personally, said
these things take time. I ran

from his apartment, tearing

through the lobby, gulping
cold air, screaming

at God until I could
only whisper:

I will wait.

His breath from all
the air vents,

His voice in the sky

and water. I rested
by the rocks.

★   ★   ★

Shahid witnessed
me sitting alone

there, in barely
a shawl. He measured

the soil, then spoke:

You are the Beloved,
You, Revolution.

Silver-palmed goddess—
hair falling in torrents, roses
of lips.

When you climb
the scaffold's branch

all the bewildered
lovers will wake; search,

       search the half-lit lanes.

★ ★ ★

Faiz writes:

If not to reach you was fate,
loving you was in my own hands.

Why complain, then, if my path
led to the gallows of separation?

★　★　★

I smeared lipstick on
without a mirror,

spread my scarves across
the dirtied carpet,

lay out my journals
like sacred texts.

Scissored my hair
so it fell like rain,

smothered my palms
with lotion and talc
until they silvered

at last. They told me
to stop. They told me
I was no prophetess.
But I was,

for I was wrathful.

My aunt pulled
Mina into the kitchen,

said, *Now listen closely,
and promise me you'll be strong:*

your sister has gone mad.

*   *   *

In the ward I tore
newspapers, shredded
rose petals.

Again and again, I pulled
the white sheets over
my head and waited

for Him. I sang
for three hours: love songs, Faiz,
and Ghalib—

Dying wouldn't be so bad
if I only had to do it once.

I held out my wrist
to the security guard, begged

him to arrest me.

★   ★   ★

The next morning I took
attendance. Read the headlines

out to the other patients.
Collected their water cups.

Ammi came in the evening
with a blanket and chocolates,

touched my hair, whispered
prayers to undo the knots.

She held my hand,

but I only wanted His.

*   *   *

Ghalib writes,

Though I lived on your promise,
I didn't think it was real;

or else, wouldn't I have died of happiness?

★　★　★

A new patient.
The others formed a circle
around her. She spoke

as if in a trance:

I am the American Dream. I am
the American Dream.
An old lady who always asked

everyone for quarters
giggled.

A phone call,
my father's voice:

My daughter,
you have buried
our heads in the dust.

*   *   *

Ghalib writes,

The desert hides itself in dust;
the river rubs its head on the earth before me.

* * *

After his visit, my uncle
told Ammi I had been erratic

with my eyeliner. She came
to fix it. I knew, then,

I had fallen. She showed me
his email:

It really isn't my fault, you see
if your daughter insisted

on coming to my apartment
on the fourth date.

As I stared and sipped tea,
the mirror told me:

You are without beauty.

★   ★   ★

When the mind rings
and you are in the bathroom
watching your face swell,

some realities— of marriage, of love,
of the Intellectual Revolution, of God—

thaw like soiled snow.
There are new ones now:

there is a gray
that tinges the cold. The moon
is of paper. In the water,
too many fish.

Your uncle is trying
to get you married in Pakistan—
to someone, anyone.

David is across the piano, singing:

Ten minutes ago I saw you,
to another girl.

vii. god vs. God

Mansur

Separate sacred from profane.

Separate it from its own bones,
like flesh and blood from marinated chicken.
If it still had a head,
we would be eating a corpse.

Separate the concept of corpse from dead flesh,
like love from the tales we're told.

Laila–Majnu, Shireen–Farhad
are legends because,
dear God,
our love cannot reach such heights.

If it did we would be dead, or God
or pelted with stone until we bled to dust.

Then they'd throw us looks of pity
and inquire about the tears in our collars.

You were a naked, hairy man, Mansur.
Not the Truth.

Why did you show them the light in your eyes?
Why did you let your wine–cup spill?

God

What feeble minds have held you between their fingers? Despite your
reshapings and growths and falls Manhattan's still living between banks.

your tide-fist's swell
spread calm as water,
as light, light, light

Nothing moved between the skins of earth and sky. They sank into the
darkness, traced each other's noses as though it were love.

the soft of dusk
its waist of light

how much of you moon?
how many eyes the night?

The Plaintiff

You skewered and fed your god
so he would not be seen at night.

Came to the temple in a robe
of paper.

The water was ice. No hand
                    would clasp yours.

You rowed farther.

The Beloved

God, I see your gray
cloak in the water,

your head
upon the stones,

the red clay
flowing in you

like blood, like tears.

She is standing
at the bank as lovers

scatter rose petals
before her. The river

is rushing to her
feet. She slips

out of her robe,
and you learn: You

were not sculpted
such as she.

You scatter
as she bathes in you,

fills in the universe
a God-shaped hole.

The Scaffold's Branch

I, Your mirror,
lie in shards.

When the color left
my cheeks,
You

left too.

Idol

in the smoke of altars
we shape you.

you are barely
there. each day they fell

you with a wave
before our very eyes.

they say your gray cloak
spans the city's fog, clouds

rising to a tower
of relentless water.

as the river fills with rain,
the city's candles

turn quiet. The moon, too,
rests behind clouds.

all the idols are gone,
they say.

god, how many candles
were lit in search of you, snuffed

when you were found?
they hold you still

above us,
force us to bow down.

The Gods of the Age

When they first
glimpsed Creation, it was only
      half-lit.

Half-lit,
as in, only half-clear—
that night, they discerned
      and imagined.

In the mind's waters,
a blurring,   a refraction.
There, we were brimming,
we were multitudes,

but they saw our darkness
and named us *Dark*.

viii. The Water of Life

Perhaps the mirror of the world will clear again;
perhaps, once again, our gaze will travel to the
limits of sight.
— Faiz

On Ghazal Poetry versus Natural Poetry:

Being excluded from a universe, too, is a type of dance. Still,
so often, we write of the moon.

Exotica: Three Poems

Ambrosia

He is a glass cup
in her hands;

she pours
wine, honey, and lime-

light. A thing
of beauty;

Conquest

he steals

a glance or two,
begins to stare—

she is the shape
of a woman. His

eyes are steel.
She blushes.

He moves closer,
demands her

secrets.

Domination

A cure for lust.

God-shaped Woman

What it is to dusk
her neck, its gleaming

sun. To be a slave:
the pull of light,

the chain's idle
bind. She draws

you into a tale—
she is thin, a slight

curve, and cannot
move to infinity.

You, pacing her
tower's garden, trample

the heads of poppies.
When she tells you

to climb the arc
of the cypress to fetch

her the ripe, hanging
moon,

you swoon. But once
she bends,

and her eyes candle,
you understand:

Life is a game.

Then you cannot look
at her, just as

she cannot see
herself in a mirror.

On Beauty

When I was 19, I trembled
to meet men's eyes.

Scarf, *burqa*, black
eyeliner. I was more
than Muslim,
more than beautiful,
more than sexual.

They wanted to know
what they could not
see.

★ ★ ★

The cruel beloved of Urdu
poetry slays her lovers

with glances, leaves them
to languish, rubbing

their foreheads
in her doorstep's dust. In this

intricacy is power:

I cannot lift
a suitcase, which means
I will never have to.

★ ★ ★

Joseph once wrote me poems
as Majnoon,
as the nightingale, as the prey.

I was engaged. Together,
we witnessed the snow consume
all of Ann Arbor,

picked it up in fistfuls, tossed
it up in the dark,

watched it fall like a spell.
He vowed to profess Islam,

as long as you know you're the only god
I'll ever worship.

*   *   *

We cannot exist for long
at high energy levels.

Something, somewhere,
will collapse.

The beloved must remain

cruel, or this collapse
is all the more inevitable.

★ ★ ★

You're crazy, I'd say.
Not crazy, he would reply. *Mad.*
Mad— say, as a moth.

(He had read my poems.)

Like Patty Boyd,
I became Laila. I wrote
back. It lasted, perhaps,

a month.

★ ★ ★

You see, these were not his
stories, nor Eric Clapton's.
He did not know the
meaning of *fanaa*. He could not.

*   *   *

The rose is still
as the nightingale sings.

As Majnoon howls
into the vast desert, Laila lies

on her bed, withering
in her own beauty.

As the moth circles the candle
in ecstasy, she is burning

herself down.

★   ★   ★

Perhaps there is no
such thing as the evil eye,
or such a thing as God
in love.

Why, then, do the children
throw stones at Majnoon,
at the swan in Glencoe Lake?

How is it that I cannot see a trace
of beauty in the clear water?

★   ★   ★

The lake thaws
and the winds gentle the grass,

but there is nothing in the air
to reach out and touch.

If I hadn't told him, during an episode:
You are my everything—

if I hadn't told him:
you'll never understand, you're white—

would he revolve around me,

                       beat his wings until I vanish?

   ★   ★   ★

mirror of the world
—*after Faiz*

when the crescent pierces
the soft   of it

     the afternoon bursts,

forlorn
despite its light

upon light. I ask: whose blade
               is sharpest?   who holds
                    this sky   today,

           then tomorrow?

to whom belong
the flames at night?
     is it your lovers, O Beloved,
                 or the executioners?

the breeze wakes us from the dark,
whispers:
     if the wounds are blooming,
         the roses will too.

Acknowledgments

Special thanks to the editors of these publications where the following poems first appeared:

A Dozen Nothing: "the branch" & "On Courting Calamity"

America Is Not The World Anthology: "Mansur"

Anomaly: "On Ghazal Poetry and Natural Poetry," "The first three weeks of war" & "Asymptote"

Best American Poetry: "Subh-e-firaaq: Morning of Separation," "Exotica: Three Poems," "On Beauty," "January 9th, 2008," "Throne"

Gulf Coast: "God-shaped Woman"

ISACOUSTIC: "Farhad the Mountain Carver" & "To Heaven"

Los Angeles Review of Books: "Ah!"

Muse/A: "Mumtaz Sahib of the Round Glasses"

Poem-A-Day: "The Gods of the Age"

Poets House: "When in the dark/ my mind brightened"

Rose Red Review: "Episode"

Salamander Magazine: "A Robe of this World," "for Majnoon," "The Coming of Spring," & "The Scaffold's Branch"

Santa Ana River Review: "Of Water"

Solstice: "for Qays"

Stirring: "For J.R." & "You're getting older, and there are such few boys"

The Friday Influence: "God" & "5 Poems"

The Margins: "Fanaa: End of Self"

Tupelo Quarterly: "The Beloved," "The night of the fourteenth," "Kathak: The Dance of the Courtesans," "the mosque an eyebrow, the tavern an eye," "mirror of the world"

Washington Square Review: "If It Were"

What Is Not Beautiful (Glass Poetry Press, 2018): "God-shaped Woman"

My eternal gratitude to my friends and mentors who have read this manuscript again and again, offering their constant and tireless support, advice, and friendship: José Angel Araguz, Emily Moore, Rajiv Mohabir, and Faisal Mohyuddin. I want to especially thank Christopher Lucka, for reading and offering advice on individual poems, and Katie Willingham, for the immense amount of work and thought she put into helping me with revisions. These are the heroes of this book, without whom it would not exist.

I am also grateful to Tupelo Press, the Helen Zell Writers' Program, Poets House, Kundiman, Glass Poetry Press, and the Asian American Writers' Workshop for supporting and nurturing my work, and to my professors, teachers, and mentors Dawud Wharnsby, Gabriela Ilieva, Amber West, r. erica doyle, Tarfia Faizullah, Victor Mendoza, A. Van Jordan, Linda Gregerson, Khaled Mattawa, and Laura Kasischke.

I would also like to thank Jessica Newman, David Hornibrook, Lauren Clark, Baqar Mehdi, Kerry Garfinkel, Malcolm Tariq, Samiah Haque, Nkosi Nkululeko, Marwa Helal, Sahar Romani, Francis Santana, Ted Kelly, John Buckley, Derrick Austin, Shadab Zeest Hashmi, Raza Ali Hasan, Sham-e-Ali Nayeem, Nisha Nusrath, Cathy Linh Che, Zara Khadeeja Majoka, Sahar Muradi, Zohra Saed, Lauren Prastien, Phoebe Petersen, Kat Finch, Ali Hassan, Anthony Frame, Tanzila Chaudhry, Aria Fani, and Suzanne Wulach for being sources of light in my life, and for encouraging me as a poet.

I owe so much to Tahira Naqvi for showing me the beauty of the world of Urdu poetry, to Frances Pritchett and Saleem Ibrahim for guiding me through its philosophical and intellectual heights, to Ustad Salamat Ali and Azra Riaz for teaching me to sing and become a vessel for the ghazal, to Saiyid Ali Naqvi for his insights on translation, and to Peter Chelkowski for his translations of Nizami's stories from the Persian. To all of them for teaching me the meaning of *fanaa*.

Lastly, my endless love to Ammi, Abbu, Munoo, Haris, and Isha, and the Ibrahim family— Bilal, Ali, Sana, Rida, Saleem Khaloo, and Sara Khala— who have lived this manuscript with me. And to Willem, for the wonder and beauty he has brought into my life since. If the mirror of this world has started to clear, if my gaze has lifted towards the limits of sight, it is because of you.

Notes

The City of the Beloved

The phrase was suggested as a title by my teacher and mentor Dr. Emily Moore.

★ ★ ★

the mosque an eyebrow, the tavern an eye

The title draws from a verse by Ghalib:

There should be a tavern under the mosque's shadow,
an eye near the brow to provide our needs.

★ ★ ★

Farhad the Mountain Carver

The legend of Shireen Khosrow (or Shireen Farhad, depending on which love story one places emphasis) is partly one of love-rivalry. This story, though originally rendered by 12th Century poet Nizami Ganjavi, varies from region to region. It begins with the romance of Shireen, an Armenian Princess, and Khosrow, a Sasanian king. According to legend, Khosrow has a dream in which his grandfather reveals to him that the immensely beautiful Shireen is his destined love. Khosrow has never seen her, but hears high praise of her beauty; his friend Shapur, who travels widely, tells him of her enchanting face, likening it to a wild rose. At this, Khosrow grows determined to win Shireen's love. He commissions Shapur to paint portraits of him and hang them around the forest where Shireen is picnicking with her friends. Shireen sees the portraits and falls feverishly in love with Khosrow, and the two, after myriad ordeals— some of which involve Khosrow's unfaithfulness— are eventually married.

The poems in this book focus on the part of the story following the entrance of the mountain-carver, Farhad. When Farhad first meets Shireen, she is living alone, her palace situated in a climate that depresses her, miserable from Khosrow's neglect and faithlessness. Overcome by her beauty, Farhad falls deeply in love with her and begins to court her with a devotion no less passionate than worship. When Khosrow comes to learn of Farhad's love for Shireen, he sets him the impossible task of carving a channel of milk leading to Shireen's palace, confident Farhad will fail. In the hope of being united with Shireen, Farhad accepts the challenge and begins to carve with incredible skill and fervor. As time passes, word spreads far and wide of his prowess, and Khosrow begins to grow alarmed the mountain-carver will complete the task. He decides to send a messenger to give Farhad false news of Shireen's death. Without thinking to first confirm the news, Farhad throws himself from the mountain, grief-stricken.

★ ★ ★

Fanaa: End of Self

The legend of Laila Majnoon is a semi-historical 7th century Arab story also rendered in Persian by Nizami Ganjavi. This tale, too, has since been adapted to many cultures, and thus exists in many retellings. My poems likely draw from a number of these in addition to Nizami's, if unconsciously.

According to legend, Laila and Qays fall obsessively in love with one another, but are forbidden by Laila's father to meet. Unable to bear the anguish of separation, Qays runs through streets and bazaars, crying out Laila's name and composing love poems for her. He loses all consciousness of the world, including his physical appearance— dust starts to cake his face, his hair grows wild, and he tears his collar in grief. The townsfolk begin to ridicule him, calling him *Majnoon*: mad, or possessed by djinns. They stone him and force him into exile.

Majnoon is left to roam the deserts and wildernesses, and he proclaims his love into their vast expanse. Meanwhile, Laila is forcibly married off to a man of noble family. Even as the two lovers are separated, they are able to communicate through an old man who carries messages between them. In one version of the story, when Laila sends a letter, Majnoon eats it because he knows what it will say. So fierce is their connection that when Laila's husband stabs Majnoon, Laila, too, collapses to death.

The legend of Laila Majnoon inspired the song "Layla" by Derek & the Dominos. Eric Clapton wrote the song for Patty Boyd, who was married to George Harrison at the time. She left him for Clapton three years later.

Some of the images I have used to describe Majnoon— particularly in the lines *"Dust on his head, blood/ on his sleeve, he danced"* are drawn from Faiz's poem

"Let us today enter the bazaar in shackles," which also contains the epigraph that begins this book. Faiz composed the poem as a political prisoner, jailed for charges of sedition against the Pakistani government. He wrote this poem after an incident when was taken from the Lahore Jail through the city on horse cart, in chains.

The phrase "death is not so cruel"— that occurs in both this poem as well as "for Majnoon," draws from these lines from the 1976 film *Laila Majnu:*

> *Death may be cruel, but it cannot perform such cruelty:*
> *while Qays lives, Laila cannot die.*

★ ★ ★

Hourglass

The concept of the "heart's throne," also present in "Asymptote," is from José Angel Araguz's poem "Stream" from his collection *Everything We Think We Hear.*

★ ★ ★

Mansur the Heretic

Mansur al-Hallaj was a 10th Century Sufi mystic who, in a state of spiritual ecstasy, is said to have proclaimed "*ana al-Haqq,*" or "I am Truth," thus claiming one of God's divine attributes. On another occasion, he declared "There is nothing in my cloak but God." Mansur also spoke of circling "the ka'bah of one's heart," referring to the seven required circumambulations of Islam's holiest site during Hajj. For his statements, considered blasphemous and heretical by the religious orthodoxy, he was executed.

The recurring image of Revolution standing at the scaffold— with red lips, silver hands, and hair falling in torrents— comes from Faiz's poem "We Who Were Murdered in Dark Lanes." My writing is particularly influenced by Agha Shahid Ali's translation of the poem in *The Rebel's Silhouette* and his reference to it in "Homage to Faiz Ahmed Faiz" from *The Half-Inch Himalayas.*

★ ★ ★

for Majnoon

The phrase "The Gods of the Age," is a translation of the phrase "Zamaane ke khudaao" from the song "Do not throw stones at my mad lover" in the 1976 film *Laila Majnu*.

★ ★ ★

for Qays

This poem draws from Mirza Sauda's famous ghazal "All that has befallen me."

★ ★ ★

If It Were

The two italicized lines in "If It Were" are from a Ghalib ghazal: "I was not fated to be united with my beloved." The title draws from the refrain, "*hotaa*."

★ ★ ★

Episode

The third stanza refers to an incident mentioned in the Qur'an about Zulekha, the Aziz's wife who lusted after the prophet Yusuf, or Joseph. When other women began to whisper about her infatuation, she invited them all to her home, and handed them all apples and knives. She then ordered Yusuf to come out into the gathering. Overcome and distracted by his beauty, all the women cut themselves instead.

★ ★ ★

On Courting Calamity

This poem draws from N.M. Rashid's poems "The Age is God" and "Are You Afraid of Life?"

Mumtaz Sahib of the Round Glasses

This poem is for Mumtaz Hussain, a prominent filmmaker and writer in the Pakistani- American community.

★ ★ ★

Ah!

This poem is based on the verse that begins the section. "Ah" is also the translation and onomatopoeia of the word "sigh" in Urdu, and the word which begins the verse.

★ ★ ★

A Robe of this World

The title is a translation of "libaas-e-majaaz," a phrase from a ghazal by Allama Iqbal. The phrase "musk-scented, rose-colored/ wine of heaven" comes from this verse by Ghalib:

> *The reason we hold heaven so dear—*
> *isn't it that rose-colored, musk-scented wine?*

★ ★ ★

The Coming of Spring

The title is a variation on Faiz's poem title "Spring has come." The phrase "The patient smiled/just once before death" is influenced by Agha Shahid Ali's translation of Faiz's poem "Verses." The image of "the bloodied feet washed/ in the water" and hennaed toes is taken from Faiz's poem "Wash your feet of blood."

★ ★ ★

102 *Shahr-e-jaanaan: The City of the Beloved*

For J.R.

The italicized verse from is from "phir aa'inah-e-'aalam," a ghazal by Faiz. This is the same ghazal from which the verse in the epigraph of the "Water of Life" section is drawn, as well as the title of "mirror of the world."

★ ★ ★

Shahr-e-jaanaan: The City of the Beloved

The first italicized section was influenced by Agha Shahid Ali's translation of Faiz's "We Who Were Murdered In Dark Lanes."

★ ★ ★

Exotica

This poem was composed with the help of Willem van der Mei, who separated the poem into three parts and gave them titles.

★ ★ ★

On Beauty

The stories of Laila-Majnoon, Shireen-Farhad, and Mansur embody the Sufi mystical concept of *fanaa:* annihilation of the ego in the path of love. *Fanaa* is the highest form of love— a state in which the devotee loses all worldly concern or desire for life, destroying his own Self in his hope to unite with the beloved. In these stories, humans are exalted to God's station, transforming into His physical manifestations. Both Majnoon and Farhad hold such feverish passion for their beloveds that they begin to worship them. Mansur feels so close to God that he *becomes* God.

★ ★ ★

mirror of the world

I composed this poem on the eve of the 2018 Midterm Elections in the U.S., and in the wake of the anti-blasphemy protests in Pakistan. The italicized lines in the poem are influenced by Agha Shahid Ali's translation of Faiz's "The harvest of silence is here."